Baby Blues® 17 Scrapbook

NEVER A DRY MOMENT

Baby Blues® 17 Scrapbook

NEVER A DRY MOMENT

by Rick Kirkman & Jerry Scott

Andrews McMeel
Publishing

Kansas City

03 04 05 06 07 BBG 10 9 8 7 6 5 4 3 2 1

ISBN: 0-7407-3304-4

Library of Congress Control Number: 2002113731

Find *Baby Blues*® on the Web at
www.babyblues.com.

——— **ATTENTION: SCHOOLS AND BUSINESSES** ———

Andrews McMeel books are available at quantity discounts with bulk purchase for educational, business, or sales promotional use. For information, please write to: Special Sales Department, Andrews McMeel Publishing, 4520 Main Street, Kansas City, Missouri 64111.

BUNNY IS HAVING TWINS!!

WOW! THAT'S REALLY GREAT... I MEAN, GOOD? I MEAN, NICE? I MEAN...

...UH...

I'M SUPPOSED TO BE GLAD, RIGHT?

YOU'RE HOPELESS, I'M CALLING YOLANDA.

BUNNY IS HAVING TWINS?

SHE TOLD ME SO TODAY!

TWINS! WOW! SHE'S REALLY GOING TO HAVE HER HANDS FULL!

THE POOR THING WILL BE A MESS FOR A WHILE.

I'M GOING TO WANT PICTURES OF THIS.

IT'S LIKE A DREAM COME TRUE, ISN'T IT?

NO DOLLS ALLOWED IN MY TRUCKS, ZOE!

FINE!

JUST FOR THAT, I'M NEVER GOING TO SPEAK TO YOU AGAIN!

YES!

THAT'S A PUNISHMENT, NOT A GIFT!

OKAY, LET'S PRACTICE WHAT YOU'RE GOING TO SAY ABOUT YOUR TRUCK FOR SHOW & TELL ONE MORE TIME.

PRETEND THAT I'M THE TEACHER...

WHAT CAN YOU TELL THE CLASS ABOUT YOUR TRUCK, HAMMIE?

IT'S A 1953 KENWORTH BULLNOSE TANDEM-AXLE WRECKER WITH DOUBLE-BOOM TOWING BARS AND CHAIN HOOKS.

PERFECT!

HAMMIE MacPHERSON?

WHAT CAN YOU TELL THE CLASS ABOUT YOUR TRUCK, HAMMIE?

IT'S MINE!!!

WHAT'S THAT STUFF?

IT'S A SPECIAL CREAM THAT I RUB ON MY TUMMY SO I WON'T GET THOSE LITTLE RED STRETCH MARKS FROM BEING PREGNANT.

YOU MEAN, LIKE THAT ONE?

UH...YEAH,

AND THAT ONE?
AND THAT ONE?
AND THAT ONE?
AND THAT ONE?
AND THAT ONE?
AND THAT ONE?
AND THAT ONE?

DID ANYONE ELSE JUST SEE A JAR OF STRETCH MARK CREAM GO FLYING BY JUST NOW?

BRAXTON-HICKS?

NOPE.

ZOE-HAMMIE.

DAD! SAY "KNOCK-KNOCK."

KNOCK-KNOCK.

KNOCK-KNOCK.
KNOCK-KNOCK.
KNOCK-KNOCK.

KNOCK-KNOCK.
KNOCK-KNOCK.
KNOCK-KNOCK.

KNOCK-KNOCK.

HAMMIE, I SAID, "KNOCK-KNOCK..." IS THERE A JOKE THAT GOES WITH THIS?

KNOCK-KNOCK.

KNOCK-KNOCK IT OFF,

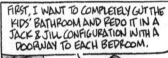

18

YOU KNOW WHAT WE SHOULD DO? START A MOMMY-TO-BE EXERCISE GROUP!

WHAT A GREAT IDEA!

WE COULD MEET AT THE PARK AFTER WE DROP THE KIDS OFF AT SCHOOL AND WALK FOR AN HOUR.

I'M IN.

YEAH! WHY DON'T WE START BY WALKING FIVE MILES A DAY, THEN WORK UP TO EIGHT OR TEN, ADD SOME WEIGHT TRAINING, AEROBICS, YOGA...

KIRKMAN & SCOTT

BUNNY, WE'RE JUST TRYING TO STAY IN SHAPE THROUGH OUR PREGNANCIES, NOT TRAIN FOR A BIATHLON.

SAID THE WOMAN WHO'S NOT HAVING TWINS.

READY?

I AM!

LET'S GO!

LET THE FIRST PREGGO POWER-WALKING SESSION BEGIN!

KIRKMAN & SCOTT

OOF! UNH! UNH!

MAKE THAT, THE FIRST SINGLE-FILE PREGGO POWER-WALKING SESSION... PASS IT ON.

IS YOUR FAMILY STILL EXCITED ABOUT THIS PREGNANCY, WANDA?

OH SURE. THEY TALK ABOUT IT ALL THE TIME.

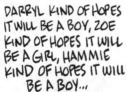

DARRYL KIND OF HOPES IT WILL BE A BOY, ZOE KIND OF HOPES IT WILL BE A GIRL, HAMMIE KIND OF HOPES IT WILL BE A BOY...

KIRKMAN & SCOTT

WHAT ABOUT YOU?

I KIND OF HOPE IT WILL BE THE LAST.

HOW FAR DO YOU THINK WE WALKED TODAY?

LET ME THINK...

WE COVERED CHILDHOOD VACCINATIONS, SIBLING RIVALRY, SWOLLEN ANKLES, SPIDER VEINS AND CLOTH vs. DISPOSABLE DIAPERS...

...I'D SAY ABOUT TWO MILES.

IF THE SUBJECT OF LABOR AND DELIVERY EVER COMES UP, WE COULD DO A MARATHON!

MOM!

ZOE, IT'S SO ANNOYING WHEN YOU JUST SIT THERE AND YELL FOR ME! GET UP AND COME INTO THE ROOM WHERE I AM.

SORRY.

MOM!!

I DON'T KNOW... I'D SAY THAT WAS EVEN MORE ANNOYING.

NOW HOW MANY MORE WEEKS UNTIL THE BABY IS BORN?

UM...ABOUT 24 WEEKS.

IS THAT A SHORT TIME, OR A LONG TIME?

IT'S A SHORT TIME THAT SEEMS LIKE A LONG TIME.

RATS!

HEY! HOW DO YOU THINK I FEEL?

21

WHERE ARE WE GOING?

HAMMIE HAS A DOCTOR'S APPOINTMENT.

WHY? WHAT'S WRONG WITH HIM?

NOTHING IS WRONG WITH HIM! IT'S JUST A CHECK-UP!

YEAH! IT'S JUST A CHECK-UP!

OH, A CHECK-UP. GOTCHA'. I UNDERSTAND.

"CHECK-UP" IS DOCTOR-TALK FOR "SHOTS," RIGHT?

AAUGGH!

HI. HAMMIE MacPHERSON TO SEE DR. JOSEPH.

HI. OKAY. PLEASE HAVE A SEAT.

IT'LL BE A FEW MINUTES, DR. JOSEPH IS RUNNING A LITTLE BEHIND TODAY.

A LITTLE BEHIND HUH...?

THAT SOUNDS LIKE A GOOD PLACE FOR A KID TO GET A SHOT, IF YOU ASK ME.

YAAAAAAAA!

KNOCK IT OFF, ZOE.

HI EVERYBODY.

HAMMIE, YOU REMEMBER DR. JOSEPH, DON'T YOU?

MAYBE.

AND HOW ARE YOU, ZOE?

FINE.

ACTUALLY, I'M GREAT, I FEEL REALLY GOOD, REALLY **REALLY** GOOD! IN FACT, I DON'T THINK I'VE EVER FELT BETTER IN MY WHOLE LIFE!

HAMMIE ISN'T GOING TO GET A SHOT TODAY, ZOE.

OH. IN THAT CASE, I'M JUST FINE.

23

BABY BLUES®

RICK KIRKMAN / JERRY SCOTT

YOU HAVEN'T EVER WORN THIS SHIRT, HAVE YOU, HAMMIE?

NO.

I THINK WE BOUGHT IT TO GO WITH THESE ADORABLE PLEATED KHAKIS, REMEMBER?

YEAH.

AND WHEN YOU PUT IT ALL TOGETHER WITH THE MATCHING STRIPED SOCKS, THE LEATHER MOCCASINS, THE CLOTH BELT, AND THE CUTE LITTLE JACKET AND HAT...

...IT'S AN ADORABLE LITTLE OUTFIT!

YEAH!

DO YOU LIKE IT?

I DON'T KNOW... LET ME TRY IT OUT.

TWICK OR TWEAT!

BWA-HA-HA HA-HA-HA-HA!

KIRKMAN & SCOTT

IT'S PERFECT.

HOW COME YOU'RE MAKING A HALLOWEEN COSTUME FOR HAMMIE, AND NOT ME?

BABY BLUES®

BY RICK KIRKMAN / JERRY SCOTT

THE BABY BLUES EMERGENCY MOTHER'S DAY CARD

FOR THOSE OF YOU WHO SOMEHOW FORGOT TO GET A MOTHER'S DAY CARD FOR THE MOM (OR MOMS) IN YOUR LIFE, BABY BLUES COMES TO THE RESCUE! SIMPLY CUT ALONG THE DOTTED LINE AND EITHER PASTE IT OVER AN OLD CARD (YOU CHEAPSKATE, YOU) OR SLIP IT ONTO THE TRAY OF EGGS BENEDICT YOU'RE ABOUT TO LOVINGLY PREPARE FOR HER BREAKFAST IN BED. NOW, **GO!**

M IS FOR THE MACARONI
YOU'VE COOKED UP BY THE TON
WITH POWDERED CHEESE, MILK & BUTTER
A GASTRONOMIC HOME RUN.

O IS FOR THE ORIFICES
YOU'VE SWABBED & DABBED & SCOURED
MILK MOUSTACHES, RUNNY NOSES
AND BOTTOMS FRESHLY FLOURED.

t IS FOR THE TIME YOU SPEND
PRODDING US SO GENTLY
TO ALWAYS BE OUR BETTER SELVES
(IT'S WORKING, INCIDENTALLY).

H IS FOR THE HOMEWORK HELP
YOU'VE GIVEN SELFLESSLY.
IF SCHOOLS GRADED ENCOURAGEMENT,
YOU'D HAVE A PhD.

e IS FOR THE EAR DRUMS
YOU'VE SACRIFICED SO FREELY
AT BIRTHDAY PARTIES & PLAY DATES
WHERE KIDS GET LOUD AND SQUEALY.

R IS FOR THE RABBIT
WHO TOOK US BY SURPRISE
EACH TIME THE DOCTOR BROKE THE NEWS
OF ITS FIGURATIVE DEMISE.

PUT THE LETTERS IN A ROW
AND TAKE A LOOK ONCE MORE.
TOGETHER THEY SPELL A NAME WE LOVE
FOR THE WOMAN WE ADORE.

LO♥E _____

KIRKMAN & SCOTT

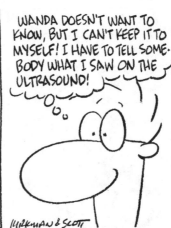

28

I SAW THAT THE BABY IS A BOY DURING THE ULTRASOUND, AND I CAN'T TELL WANDA BECAUSE SHE SAID THAT SHE DOESN'T WANT TO KNOW!

MAYBE IF I JUST GAVE HER A HINT, SOMETHING SUBTLE...

BOY, OH BOY, OH BOY, OH BOY, OH BOY, OH BOY, OH BOY, OH BOY, OH BOY, OH BOY! GREAT ULTRASOUND, HUH?

ARE YOU TRYING TO TELL ME SOMETHING?

OH BOY.

KIRKMAN & SCOTT

;GASP!; YOU KNOW THE SEX OF THE BABY, AND YOU'RE NOT TELLING ME!

I'M NOT TELLING YOU BECAUSE YOU SAID YOU DON'T WANT TO KNOW!

I DON'T WANT TO KNOW, BUT I DON'T WANT TO NOT KNOW IF YOU KNOW... YOU KNOW??

I KNOW! I DON'T WANT YOU TO NOT KNOW WHAT I KNOW, TOO!

SO, WHAT DO YOU KNOW?

I'LL TELL YOU AS SOON AS I FIGURE OUT WHAT WE JUST SAID TO EACH OTHER.

KIRKMAN & SCOTT

LOOK, I CHANGED MY MIND. DON'T TELL ME, OKAY?

REALLY?

YEAH. EVEN IF YOU DO THINK YOU KNOW THE SEX OF THE BABY, JUST KEEP IT TO YOURSELF, CAN YOU DO THAT FOR ME?

SURE.

REALLY?

KIRKMAN & SCOTT

HOW COULD YOU KEEP A SECRET LIKE THAT FROM YOUR OWN WIFE??

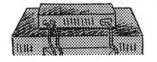

36

37

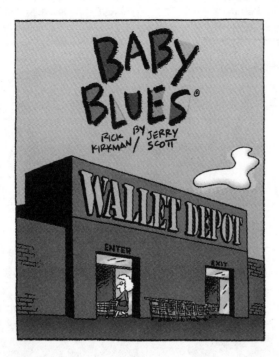

45

I AM SO EXCITED ABOUT GOING TO DAY CAMP!

AND HAMMIE AND I ARE EXCITED ABOUT SPENDING THE DAY TOGETHER, AREN'T WE HAMMIE?

ZOE WILL BE OFF HAVING FUN WITH HER FRIENDS WHILE YOU AND I ARE HAVING FUN HERE AT HOME!

YEAH! LOTS OF FUN! LOTS AND LOTS AND LOTS AND LOTS...

KEESHA'S MOM IS HERE TO PICK ME UP! BYE!

...AND LOTS AND LOTS AND LOTS AND LOTS OF FUN!

THIS BETTER BE GOOD.

KIRKMAN & SCOTT

BYE, ZOE! HAVE A GREAT TIME AT DAY CAMP!

WELL, YOU HAVE THE WHOLE DAY TO YOURSELF, HAMMIE.

KIRKMAN & SCOTT

NO BIG SISTER TO TEASE YOU...NO BIG SISTER TO SHARE YOUR TOYS WITH...NO BIG SISTER TO BOSS YOU AROUND...YOU CAN DO WHATEVER YOU WANT!

YEAH!

WHAT DO YOU WANT TO DO FIRST?

WATCH FOR ZOE TO COME HOME.

WHEN IS ZOE GONNA' BE HOME?

HER DAY CAMP IS OVER AT THREE O'CLOCK.

IS THAT A LONG TIME, OR A SHORT TIME?

TO A BOY WITH A BAD ATTITUDE, IT'LL SEEM LIKE A LONG TIME, BUT TO A BOY WITH A GOOD ATTITUDE, IT'LL SEEM LIKE A SHORT TIME.

OH.

KIRKMAN & SCOTT

WHO'S THIS SECOND KID YOU'RE TALKING ABOUT?

46

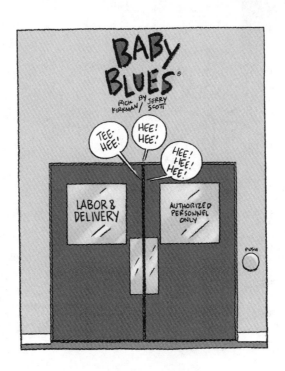

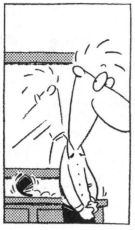

FLAP FLAP FLAP FLAP

FOR SOME REASON, A BUNCH OF MONEY JUST FLEW OUT OF MY WALLET!

WOW. LOOK! THE KIDS JUST GOT INVITED TO FOUR MORE BIRTHDAY PARTIES.

A CHAUFFEURED LIMO TO THE SCIENCE-ATERIUM? A PRIVATE POOL PARTY AT THE COUNTRY CLUB? A TRAIL RIDE AT KID-E-RANCH?

WOW.

THESE SOUND LIKE SOME PRETTY HIGH-END BIRTHDAY PARTIES.

NO KIDDING.

WHAT'S THE MINIMUM BUY-IN?

IF I STAY AND VOLUNTEER TO HELP OUT, MAYBE $15 A PRESENT. IF I DON'T, $20 EACH.

FOUR BIRTHDAY PARTIES TIMES $15-A-GIFT MEANS THAT WE'RE OUT SIXTY BUCKS FOR PRESENTS??

NOT NECESSARILY.

SOMETIMES I BUY THINGS AND PUT THEM IN MY "PRESENT STASH" FOR LAST-MINUTE GIFTS.

A BABY SPICE DOLL AND A SQUID BEANIE BABY?

I GUESS IT'S BEEN A WHILE SINCE I'VE PUT ANYTHING INTO THE OL' PRESENT STASH.

IN OTHER WORDS, WE'RE OUT SIXTY BUCKS **PLUS** THE COST OF THIS JUNK.

ZOE, WHAT DO YOU THINK SKYE WOULD LIKE FOR HER BIRTHDAY?

UM...

HMMM...

WHICH ONE IS SKYE? IS SHE THE GIRL WHO'S ALWAYS MEAN TO ME, OR THE ONE WHO CALLED YOU "FATSO"?

HOW ABOUT SOMETHING FROM THE BARGAIN BIN?

I THINK SKYE WOULD WANT THIS FOR HER BIRTHDAY.

I KNOW BECAUSE I REALLY, REALLY, REALLY, REALLY WANT ONE MYSELF.

THAT'S SWEET, ZOE. THEN, OF COURSE, WE'LL BUY THIS!

ONLY ONE?

I CAN'T WAIT 'TIL SKYE'S BIRTHDAY PARTY!

SKYE SAID THERE'S GOING TO BE GAMES AND SWIMMING AND HOT DOGS AND EVERYTHING!

WITH TAX, THAT'LL BE $29.94.

29 BUCKS??

EAT LOTS OF CAKE.

57

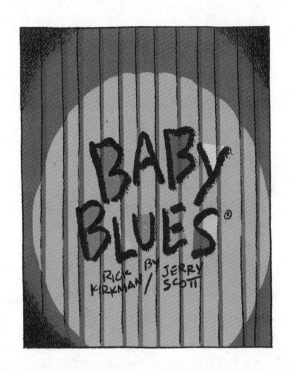

WANDA! WHAT ARE YOU DOING?

POKING THIS MEAT TO SEE IF IT'S FRESH.

YEP. NICE AND FRESH.

DO YOU WANT ME TO PUT IT IN THE CART?

NO. GRAB THE ONE UNDERNEATH IT.

I NEVER BUY ANYTHING WITH POKE MARKS IN IT.

WANDA, YOU JUST POKED THIS PACKAGE OF MEAT, AND NOW YOU'RE NOT GOING TO BUY IT?

OF COURSE NOT. IT HAS A POKE MARK IN IT.

YEAH! FROM **YOUR** FINGER!

I'M NOT GOING TO WIN THIS ARGUMENT, AM I?

THE LONGER YOU TALK, THE SOFTER THE ICE CREAM GETS.

I DON'T KNOW, WANDA, I STILL DON'T FEEL RIGHT ABOUT YOU POKING THAT PACKAGE OF MEAT, THEN NOT BUYING IT.

I UNDERSTAND.

MAYBE YOU'RE RIGHT. MAYBE IT WAS THE WRONG THING TO DO.

MAYBE MY SHOPPING METHODS ARE A LITTLE DATED. MAYBE I NEED TO MAKE A CHANGE.

MAYBE I SHOULD DO THE GROCERY SHOPPING ALONE FROM NOW ON.

NEVER MIND! MOVING ON...!

DO WE HAVE ANY NOTEBOOK PAPER?

YES, HERE'S SOME, WHY?

I WANT TO PRACTICE MY SPELLING SO I'LL BE READY WHEN SCHOOL STARTS, SO I'M GOING TO MAKE A SUMMER JOURNAL.

ZOE, THAT'S A WONDERFUL IDEA!

YEAH. I'M GOING TO CALL IT "A SUMMER TO REMEMBER."

HOW DO YOU SPELL "A"?

KIRKMAN & SCOTT

KIRKMAN & SCOTT

I'LL BE GLAD WHEN BUNNY FINALLY HAS HER TWINS.

THOSE ARE SOME MAJOR CONTRACTIONS SHE'S HAVING OVER THERE.

RESTING UP?

SORT OF.

I'M GETTING READY TO CLEAN ZOE'S ROOM. IT LOOKS LIKE A TOY STORE THREW UP IN THERE.

HA! HA! YOU AND YOUR EXAGGERATIONS! I'LL HANDLE THIS.

KIRKMAN & SCOTT

NOW I THINK I'M GOING TO BE SICK!

TOLD YA!

66

67

AFTER I HAVE THIS BABY, I REALLY WANT TO GET BACK IN SHAPE.

I REALLY WANT TO SLIM DOWN... I REALLY WANT TO TONE UP...

GRUNT! OOF! ERF! BOOF! AAARGH!

...I REALLY WANT TO GET OUT OF A CHAIR QUIETLY AGAIN.

I WAS NEXT DOOR, AND I HEARD A BUNCH OF NOISE! ARE YOU OKAY?

HELLO?

WANDA? IT'S BUNNY. MY CONTRACTIONS HAVE STARTED!

REALLY?

YES! DO YOU REALIZE WHAT THIS MEANS?

UH, THAT YOU'RE ABOUT TO GIVE LIFE TO TWO HUMAN BEINGS?

I WAS GOING TO SAY THAT I'M ON MY WAY TO FITTING INTO MY JEANS AGAIN, BUT OKAY...

HAVE A NICE EPISIOTOMY, BUNNY.

BEEP!

BUNNY IS HAVING CONTRACTIONS.

REALLY?

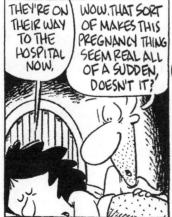
THEY'RE ON THEIR WAY TO THE HOSPITAL NOW.

WOW. THAT SORT OF MAKES THIS PREGNANCY THING SEEM REAL ALL OF A SUDDEN, DOESN'T IT?

OOF!

ERF!

BOOF!

UNH!

IT SEEMED REAL TO **SOME** OF US FOR QUITE A WHILE, NOW, PAL.

KIRKMAN & SCOTT

I'LL GO MAKE SOME TEA.

AT 2 A.M.??

DARRYL, OUR FRIEND, BUNNY, IS ON HER WAY TO THE HOSPITAL TO DELIVER TWINS! HOW CAN I GO BACK TO BED AT A TIME LIKE THIS?

YOU'RE WORRIED ABOUT HER AREN'T YOU?

NAW, SHE'LL BE FINE.

BUT I ONLY HAVE A FEW MORE HOURS OF HER BEING FATTER THAN ME, AND I'M NOT GOING TO SLEEP THROUGH THEM.

HI BUTCH. THANKS FOR CALLING... HOW'S BUNNY DOING?

PRETTY GOOD, I GUESS.

SHE'S A LITTLE UNCOMFORTABLE, SO THINGS ARE KIND OF TENSE RIGHT NOW.

MEANING THE ANESTHESIOLOGIST DOESN'T KNOW WHETHER TO GIVE PAINKILLERS TO BUNNY OR HER NURSES.

OOOOH! THAT WOMAN!

G'MORNING.

BUNNY HAD HER BABIES.

WHAT? WHEN??

ABOUT AN HOUR AGO. TWIN BOYS, JUST OVER SIX POUNDS EACH. EVERYBODY IS DOING FINE.

THAT'S SO GREAT. I'M REALLY HAPPY FOR THEM.

SHOULD WE SEND FLOWERS?

THREE BOYS IN THE SAME HOUSE? I THINK WE SHOULD SEND FOOD.

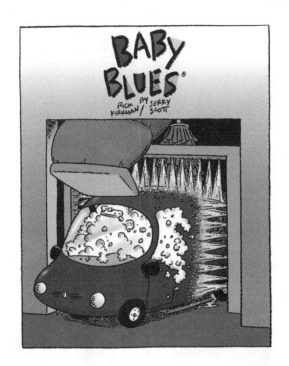

OKAY! I GIVE UP! WHERE ARE YOU?

GOOD SPOT!

I AM **NOT** A HIDING PLACE!

MOMMY, I DON'T HAVE ANY CLEAN P.J.s

OH, THAT'S RIGHT! I FORGOT TO PUT THEM IN THE DRYER!

HERE, YOU CAN WEAR ONE OF MY T-SHIRTS AS A NIGHTIE.

OKAY,

HOW'S THE FIT?

THE LENGTH IS FINE, BUT I THINK THE NECK HOLE IS TOO BIG.

DADDY, LOOK!

I GOT ONE, TOO!

WHAT'S WITH THE NEW TOYS?

GUILT PURCHASE.

THE KIDS WENT SHOPPING WITH ME, AND I WAS KIND OF SHORT-TEMPERED WITH THEM.

AND THE NEW SOCKET SET?

THAT'S FOR YOU IF YOU DON'T GIVE ME A HARD TIME ABOUT THE TOYS,

WHY DID YOU SIGN US UP FOR A LAMAZE CLASS? YOU ALREADY KNOW HOW TO HAVE A BABY.

YES, BUT IT'S BEEN THREE YEARS, AND I NEED A REFRESHER. BESIDES, IT'LL BE FUN.

DON'T THINK OF IT AS A CLASS... THINK OF IT AS A NIGHT OUT FOR US ALONE.

ISN'T THERE SOMETHING FUNDAMENTALLY WEIRD ABOUT TWO PEOPLE GOING TO A LAMAZE CLASS TO GET AWAY FROM THEIR KIDS??

DARRYL, WE'RE GOING TO A LAMAZE CLASS TOGETHER, WHETHER YOU LIKE IT OR NOT.

I SIGNED US UP FOR THURSDAYS AT SEVEN. YOLANDA IS GOING TO WATCH THE KIDS. IT'LL BE FUN AND INFORMATIVE.

END OF DISCUSSION.

FUN AND INFORMATIVE, HUH?

IF I WANT TO BE INFORMED ABOUT KIDS, I CAN JUST TRIP OVER ONE IN MY OWN LIVING ROOM... THAT'S WHAT I SHOULDA' SAID!

I HEARD THAT!

HI! I'M SYLVIA, YOUR LAMAZE INSTRUCTOR. YOU MUST BE THE MacPHERSONS!

HI.

LAMAZE

WOW... EVERYONE HERE IS SO YOUNG!

DON'T WORRY ABOUT IT. YOU'LL FIT RIGHT IN.

IT'S AN HONOR HAVING A COUPLE WITH YOUR VAST BREADTH OF EXPERIENCE IN MY CLASS!

SUDDENLY I FEEL ALL FRED MacMURRAY

NEVER SAY "VAST BREADTH" TO A WOMAN IN MATERNITY CLOTHES.

IS IT TRUE THAT THIS WILL BE YOUR **THIRD** BABY?

YEP.

SO THEN YOU'LL HAVE THREE KIDS UNDER THE AGE OF SEVEN?

UH-HUH.

WOW... THREE LITTLE ONES...

IT MUST BE LIKE LIVING IN YOUR OWN SITCOM!

YEAH. BUT WITHOUT THE LAUGH TRACK AND THE MONEY.

MMMMMMM...

SYLVIA?

...MMMMMMM

YES, DARRYL?

I'M HAVING TROUBLE WITH THE LOWER BACK MASSAGE.

GOOD BODY POSITION... KNEES LEVEL WITH THE HIPS... HANDS PRESSING INWARD...

...MMMMM...

WHAT'S THE PROBLEM?

WHENEVER I STOP, SHE GROWLS AT ME.

GRRRRR...

THAT WAS FUN!

YEAH.

IT WAS NICE TO SPEND SOME TIME TOGETHER JUST TOUCHING, MASSAGING AND RELAXING.

UM-HMMM...

IT REMINDS ME OF THE OLD PRE-KID DAYS.

IT REMINDS ME OF HOW THEY **BECAME** THE OLD PRE-KID DAYS.

BUNNY, YOU NEVER SAID WHAT YOU AND BUTCH NAMED THE TWINS.

THAT'S BECAUSE WE STILL HAVEN'T DECIDED.

WHAT??

NOTHING SOUNDS RIGHT TO US YET, SO WE DECIDED NOT TO RUSH IT.

FOR THE TIME BEING, WE'RE JUST CALLING THEM BY THE COLORS OF THEIR WRIST BANDS.

KIRKMAN & SCOTT

YOU HAVE TWIN BOYS NAMED PURPLE AND GREEN.

I PREFER PUCE AND TEAL.

BUNNY, HOW DID YOU GET THE BABIES RELEASED FROM THE HOSPITAL WITHOUT GIVING THEM NAMES?

I JUST TOLD THEM THAT WE HADN'T DECIDED, AND WE'D LET THEM KNOW WHEN WE DID.

REALLY?

THEY ALWAYS TELL YOU THAT YOU CAN'T GO HOME UNTIL THE BIRTH CERTIFICATES ARE COMPLETED, BUT IT'S NOT TRUE.

NNH! NNH!

WELL, I SURE BELIEVED THEM.

YEAH....

...I FIGURED THERE MUST BE AN EXPLANATION FOR "HAMMIE."

KIRKMAN & SCOTT

AT FIRST I THOUGHT WE SHOULD GIVE THE TWINS NAMES THAT ARE SIGNIFICANT TO THE NIGHT THEY WERE CONCEIVED.

THAT'S INTERESTING.

Z Z

BUTCH AND I HAD WATCHED "THE AFRICAN QUEEN" THE NIGHT I GOT PREGNANT THE FIRST TIME, SO NATURALLY WE NAMED OUR BABY BOY BOGART.

HOW ROMANTIC!

KIRKMAN & SCOTT

BUT I DON'T THINK IT'S GOING TO WORK NOW.

WHY? WHAT MOVIE DID YOU SEE THIS TIME?

Z Z

DUMB AND DUMBER.

OOH

Z Z

81

I'VE BEEN HOME FOR SIXTY SECONDS AND I'M ALREADY TIRED.

MULTIPLY THAT BY 180 MINUTES AND YOU'LL HAVE AN IDEA WHAT THIS AFTERNOON HAS BEEN LIKE.

MR. DOYLE? MR. DOYLE? MR. DOYLE?

ZOE, IT'S A SMALL CLASSROOM. I CAN SEE YOU.

IF YOU WANT TO GET MY ATTENTION, JUST RAISE YOUR HAND. THERE'S NO NEED TO USE YOUR VOICE, TOO.

I DON'T KNOW IF I CAN DO THAT...

...MY HANDS AND MOUTH SORT OF WORK AS A TEAM.

WHERE'S HAMMIE?

HE'S IN HIS ROOM PLAYING WITH BLOCKS.

GOOD. EVEN HAMMIE CAN'T GET INTO MUCH TROUBLE PLAYING WITH BLOCKS.

IF YOU SAY SO.

85

MOMMY-TO-BE, HUH?

YES.

BLEEP! BLEEP!

YOUR FIRST?

WHAT'S THE DUE DATE?

MY THIRD, OCTOBER 26th.

BLEEP!

BOY OR A GIRL?

WE DON'T KNOW.

BLEEP! BLEEP!

VAGINAL DELIVERY OR CAESAREAN?

HAVE WE MET???

BLEEP!

KIRKMAN & SCOTT

ZOE! DON'T SLOUCH! SIT LIKE A LADY AT THE TABLE!!

I AM! SEE?

NO, YOU'RE NOT! YOU'RE — WHAT?

OH

PREGNANT LADIES DON'T COUNT.

COUNT FOR WHAT?

KIRKMAN & SCOTT

86

 YOU NEVER REALLY KNOW HOW NOSY AND PERSONAL SOME PEOPLE CAN BE UNTIL YOU'RE PREGNANT.

 TODAY IN THE GROCERY STORE, SOME WOMAN ASKED ME IF I WAS GOING TO BREAST-FEED, ANOTHER WOMAN WANTED TO TOUCH MY TUMMY, AND THE CHECKOUT CLERK ASKED ME IF I WAS PLANNING A VAGINAL OR CAESAREAN DELIVERY!

KIRKMAN & SCOTT

 WHATEVER HAPPENED TO PERSONAL PRIVACY?? DON'T GET UPSET. IT AGGRAVATES YOUR HEMORRHOIDS, REMEMBER?

 I'M SERIOUS, DARRYL! I'M SICK OF TOTAL STRANGERS TREATING ME LIKE A SIDESHOW FREAK!

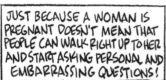 JUST BECAUSE A WOMAN IS PREGNANT DOESN'T MEAN THAT PEOPLE CAN WALK RIGHT UP TO HER AND START ASKING PERSONAL AND EMBARRASSING QUESTIONS! EXCUSE ME...

 I'M EIGHT MONTHS PREGNANT, IT'S MY THIRD CHILD, YES, I'M GOING TO BREAST-FEED, AND, NO, THE STRETCH MARKS NEVER GO AWAY! IS THERE ANYTHING ELSE YOU'D LIKE TO KNOW???

 ACTUALLY, I WAS JUST GOING TO ASK YOU TO PUT THIS IN THE MAILBOX, BUT I THINK I CHANGED MY MIND.

87

WHAT ARE YOU MAKING THERE, HAMMIE?

A CARD FOR MY PRE-KINDERGARTEN TEACHER.

WE SET A NEW RECORD TODAY.

A RECORD? WHAT KIND OF RECORD?

BY THE TIME THE TEACHER GOT THE CLASS SETTLED DOWN ENOUGH TO TAKE ATTENDANCE, IT WAS TIME TO GO HOME.

NOW WRITE, "I HOPE YOUR HEADACHE GOES AWAY SOON. LOVE, HAMMIE."

GESUNDHEIT.

SNIF!

YOU HAVE TWO DIFFERENT SHOES ON.

I DO??

OH, GREAT.

THAT'S IT! IT'S OFFICIAL!

I'VE HIT ROCK-BOTTOM!

I'M WALKING AROUND IN A HUGE MATERNITY BLOUSE AND MISMATCHED SHOES... I MEAN, WHAT COULD BE MORE EMBARRASSING THAN THAT??

THEY'RE BOTH LEFT SHOES.

I'M TIRED OF BEING PREGNANT. I'M READY TO HAVE THIS BABY.

REALLY, REALLY, REALLY, REALLY, REALLY, REALLY, REALLY, REALLY, REALLY, REALLY, REALLY, REALLY READY.

ANYTHING I CAN DO TO HELP?

CAN YOU INVENT A MACHINE THAT WILL TRANSPORT ME TWO WEEKS INTO THE FUTURE TO MY DUE DATE?

NO, BUT I CAN BRING YOU A QUART OF MOCHA ALMOND FUDGE ICE CREAM.

YOU MAY NOT BE A SCIENTIFIC GENIUS, BUT YOU'RE STILL PRETTY HANDY TO HAVE AROUND.

I DO MY BEST...

I'M NEVER GOING TO HAVE THIS BABY!

MY DUE DATE IS GOING TO COME AND GO, AND I'LL STILL BE PREGNANT!

ZOE & HAMMIE WILL GRADUATE FROM COLLEGE, GET MARRIED, START FAMILIES OF THEIR OWN, AND I'LL STILL BE PREGNANT!

GLACIERS WILL MELT, MOUNTAIN RANGES WILL RISE AND ERODE, AND I WILL STILL BE PREGNANT!!

MOMMY IS OKAY, HAMMIE. SHE'S JUST A LITTLE ANXIOUS TO HAVE THE BABY.

YEAH, THE WEEK BEFORE YOU WERE BORN, ME AND DADDY HAD TO WEAR EARPLUGS.

KIRKMAN & SCOTT

CAMILLE! THAT'S A PRETTY NAME! I'M ADDING IT TO MY LIST OF GIRLS' NAMES.

YOU HAVE A LIST?

OF COURSE! FAVORITE GIRL NAMES AND FAVORITE BOY NAMES.

AND EACH LIST HAS SEVERAL SUB-CATEGORIES FOR NAMES THAT WOULD WORK WELL WITH DOMINANT FEATURES SUCH AS "HAIR COLOR," "EYE COLOR," "FULL LIPS," "BUTTON NOSE," ETC.

MY HOUSE MAY BE A MESS, BUT MY BRAIN IS TOTALLY ORGANIZED.

Z

KICK!

AAAAAAGH!

SORRY. THESE SUDDEN LEG CRAMPS ARE SO ANNOYING.

THAT MUST BE REALLY HARD FOR YOU.

MOMMY, HAVE WE EVER RENTED A STRETCH LIMO WITH A HOT TUB?

UM, NO.

ARE YOU SURE?

YES. I THINK I WOULD HAVE REMEMBERED SOMETHING LIKE THAT.

SEE?? I TOLD YOU WE WERE POOR!

KIRKMAN & SCOTT

OKAY, WE HAVE THE MUSIC, THE PILLOWS, THE HOT WATER BOTTLE, THE TENNIS BALL FOR BACK MASSAGE, AND SNACKS FOR ME.

WOW! I DIDN'T FORGET ANYTHING THIS TIME!

I GUESS AFTER A FEW KIDS, THIS BIRTHING STUFF BECOMES KIND OF ROUTINE.

GIRL.

GIRL.

BOY.

BOY.

I'M RIGHT, AND YOU KNOW IT.

I'M RIGHT, AND YOU KNOW IT.

ARE YOU SURE?

WANNA BET?

I'M POSITIVE.

NAME YOUR STAKES.

LOSER DOES THE BREAST-FEEDING FOR THE FIRST WEEK.

ON THE OTHER HAND, IT DOES FEEL A LITTLE LIKE A GIRL...

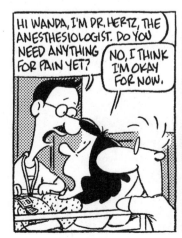

HI WANDA, I'M DR. HERTZ, THE ANESTHESIOLOGIST. DO YOU NEED ANYTHING FOR PAIN YET?

NO, I THINK I'M OKAY FOR NOW.

GOOD, THEN I'LL CHECK WITH YOU AGAIN IN A WHILE.

OKAY.

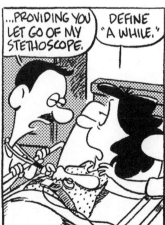

...PROVIDING YOU LET GO OF MY STETHOSCOPE.

DEFINE "A WHILE."

97

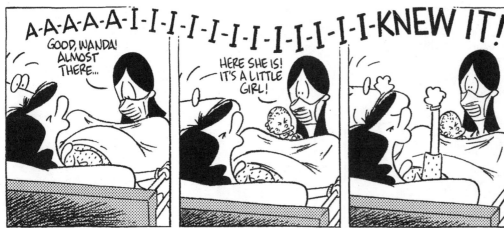

WREN??   WREN.

LIKE THE BIRD?   YES. THE ENGLISH SONGBIRD.

WREN! PUT THAT DOWN! WREN! PICK UP THOSE TOYS! EAT YOUR SUPPER, WREN!

SHORT, CUTE AND WORKS WELL WITH A HOLLER, I'M SOLD.   ♪ HELLO, WREN. ♪

WREN MacPHERSON.   WREN. I LIKE IT.

SO GENTLE, SO DELICATE, SO LYRICAL.

WHAT INSPIRED YOU TO COME UP WITH SUCH AN ELEGANT NAME?   A BIRD SMACKED INTO THE WINDOW WHILE I WAS EATING BREAKFAST.

I JUST SAW MIKE IN THE CAFETERIA. HE SAYS YOLANDA IS STILL IN LABOR.

STILL IN LABOR??   YUP. TWENTY-SEVEN HOURS AND COUNTING.

THAT'S TERRIBLE! HOW HORRIBLE!   I KNOW.

AND I BET IT'S HARD ON YOLANDA, TOO.

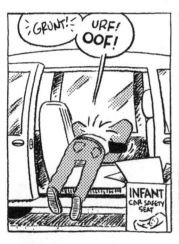

ALL SET?

I THINK SO.

IT'S A GIRL!

YOU COULD MAKE TWO TRIPS, YOU KNOW!

I GOT IT.

IT'S A GIRL!

KIRKMAN & SCOTT

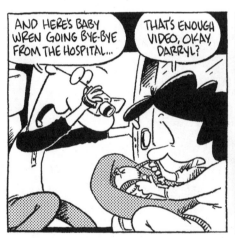

AND HERE'S BABY WREN GOING BYE-BYE FROM THE HOSPITAL...

THAT'S ENOUGH VIDEO, OKAY, DARRYL?

WHY? WE DID THIS FOR ZOE AND HAMMIE.

I KNOW, BUT I'M NOT WEARING MUCH MAKEUP AND THAT STUPID DIGITAL CAMERA CAPTURES EVERY WRINKLE AND CREASE IN MY FACE.

KIRKMAN & SCOTT

I HOPE SHE DOESN'T FEEL CHEATED SOMEDAY...

THE YOUNGEST CHILD ALWAYS HAS THE FEWEST PHOTOS BECAUSE THE YOUNGEST CHILD HAS THE OLDEST MOTHER.

OKAY, I'LL PICK UP HAMMIE FROM SCHOOL, RUN A COUPLE OF ERRANDS, PICK UP ZOE, BRING THEM BOTH HOME...

...THEN I'LL SWING BY THE OFFICE TO PICK UP SOME PAPERWORK, MEET YOUR MOM AT THE AIRPORT, GRAB SOME TAKE-OUT AND BE BACK HERE BY FIVE.

SOUNDS GOOD.

HOW CAN A 25% INCREASE IN THE SIZE OF A FAMILY MAKE THINGS **800%** MORE COMPLICATED?

YOU THINK THIS IS BAD? WAIT 'TIL WE HAVE THREE KIDS ON THREE DIFFERENT SOCCER TEAMS.

KIRKMAN & SCOTT

DARRYL MacPHERSON.

HI HONEY. IT'S WANDA.

GOOD NEWS! MY SISTER OFFERED TO PICK UP MOM AT THE AIRPORT, SO YOU DON'T HAVE TO.

REALLY? THAT'S GREAT!

NOW I CAN CATCH UP ON SOMETHING I'VE BEEN PUTTING OFF FOR THE PAST FEW DAYS.

ZZZZZZZZZZZ

HELLO? ANYBODY HOME?

GRANDMA'S HERE!

NOW REMEMBER WHAT I TOLD YOU ABOUT MANNERS.

IF GRANDMA BROUGHT YOU ANY GIFTS, SHE'LL GIVE THEM TO YOU WHEN SHE'S READY. I DON'T WANT TO HEAR "GIMMIE! GIMMIE! GIMMIE!"

GIMMIE! GIMMIE! GIMMIE!

WELL, HELLO THERE! WHO ARE YOU?

HER NAME IS WREN AND SHE'S ONLY TWO-DAYS-OLD AND SHE'S OUR SISTER AND SHE CRIES A LOT UNTIL MOMMY FEEDS HER THEN SHE GOES TO SLEEP.

I DON'T THINK SHE HAS ANY HOBBIES YET.

WELL, LET'S GIVE HER A FEW DAYS...

YOU HAD YOUR BABY?? OH, THAT'S GREAT, YOLANDA!

WE'RE ALL THRILLED FOR YOU!

BOY OR GIRL?

BOY OR GIRL?

GIRL.

YAY!

NUTS!

MAKE THAT: TWO THRILLED, ONE ABSTAINED.

YOLANDA JUST CALLED. SHE HAD HER BABY.

WHEN?

THIS MORNING.

IT'S ABOUT TIME.

YEAH! THAT WAS REAL RUDE OF HER TO STAY IN LABOR FORTY HOURS JUST FOR HER OWN SELFISH PLEASURE.

YOU KNOW WHAT I MEANT!

OH MY GOSH! WHO ARE THOSE FROM?

I DUNNO. CHECK THE CARD.

Congratulations on your new daughter! Love, Ron and Gardie

THOSE GUYS!

THEY SHOULDN'T HAVE!

BY THE WAY, WHO THE HECK ARE RON AND GARDIE?

DANG. I WAS HOPING YOU KNEW.

BABY BLUES®

RICK KIRKMAN BY JERRY SCOTT

DARRYL...?

WHAT ARE YOU DOING UP?

I WAS JUST THINKING...

FOR AS LONG AS I CAN REMEMBER, I'VE PICTURED MYSELF AS A GUY WITH A BIG FAMILY, AND NOW LOOK AT ME.

I DID IT, WANDA! I'VE ACHEIVED MY DREAM.

THANKS TO YOU, I HAVE THE UNBELIEVABLE PRIVILEGE OF SHARING THE LIFE OF YET ANOTHER BEAUTIFUL CHILD!

BBBBBWWWAAAAAAAAAAAAAAAAAAAAADAAAA!

I THINK I'LL GO CELEBRATE.

GET BACK HERE!!

BLORP!

TRASH DAY 5 YEARS AGO
2 Parents—1 Kid

TRASH DAY 3 YEARS AGO
2 Parents—2 Kids

TRASH DAY TODAY
2 Parents—3 Kids

JUST BACK IT UP TO THE FRONT DOOR AND I'LL TAKE IT FROM THERE!

KIRKMAN & SCOTT

MY DAD WILL BE HERE TOMORROW, THEN HE AND MOM WILL GO HOME ON FRIDAY.

MMMF.

IT'S BEEN SO NICE HAVING HELP WITH THE BABY. I'M REALLY GOING TO MISS HER.

HI KIDS! I DON'T WANT TO BE A BOTHER, BUT WOULD ONE OF YOU MIND SHOWING ME HOW TO USE THE TV REMOTE AGAIN?

YEAH, IT'S GOING TO BE LONELY HERE IN THE BATHROOM WHEN SHE'S GONE.

MOM! FOR HEAVEN'S SAKE!!

KIRKMAN & SCOTT

GRANDPA HUGH IS COMING TOMORROW.

WHERE IS HE GOING TO SLEEP?

WELL, IT'LL TAKE SOME SHUFFLING, BUT HE AND GRANDMA WILL SLEEP IN OUR BED, DADDY AND I WILL SLEEP ON THE SOFA BED, ZOE WILL MOVE BACK INTO HER ROOM, AND YOU AND WREN CAN STAY WHERE YOU ARE.

NO FAIR!

I WANT TO BE SHUFFLED, TOO!

KIRKMAN & SCOTT

BABY BLUES

BY RICK KIRKMAN / JERRY SCOTT

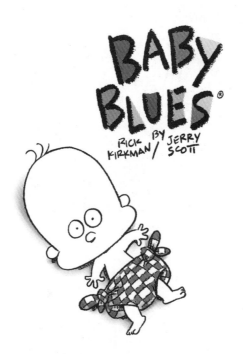

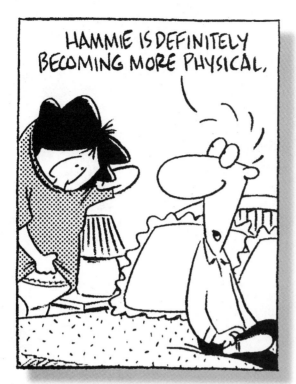

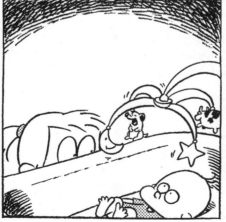

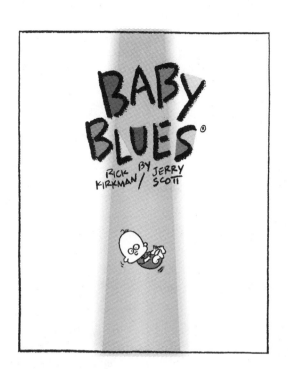

OUR BABY IS THIS YEAR'S MODEL, BUT OUR STROLLER SURE ISN'T.

DOUBLE COUPONS!

DARRYL! PUT THAT SILLY TABLOID DOWN AND HELP ME FIND THE CREAM CHEESE.

'K.

THOSE THINGS ARE JUST FULL OF JUNK THAT YOU'RE USUALLY BETTER OFF NOT KNOWING, ANYWAY.

UH-OH.

TOO LATE.

OKAY, WHICH FLAKY CELEBRITY JUST HAD A BABY, AND NAMED IT "WREN."

CAUTION

CAUTION

AUTION